PARKOUR

Written by Paul Stevenson

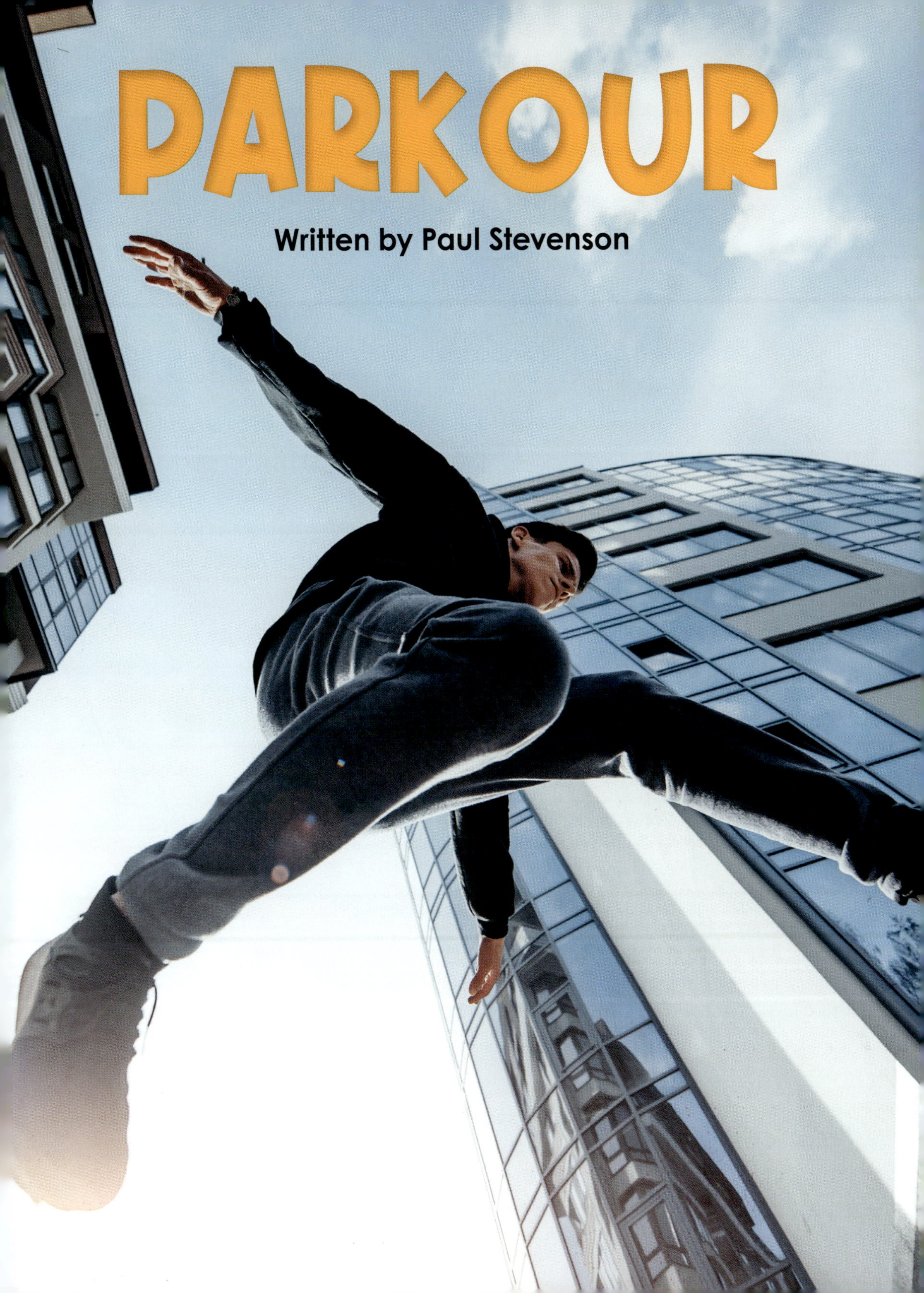

CONTENTS

First published in 2024 by
Hungry Tomato Ltd
F15, Old Bakery Studios,
Blewetts Wharf, Malpas Road,
Truro, Cornwall,
TR1 1QH, UK.

A CIP catalog record for this book is available from the British Library.

ISBN 9781915461926
Manufactured in the USA

Discover more at
www.hungrytomato.com

Neither the publisher nor the author shall be liable for any bodily harm or damage to property that may happen as a result of trying the parkour moves in this book.

DISCLAIMER:

The parkour moves featured in this book have been performed by people who are experienced professionals, or by people who have had professional training in parkour.

All words in **BOLD** can be found in the glossary.

This is... PARKOUR!

DYNAMIC, EXPLOSIVE...
POWERFUL!

Ghosting through the city. Running and leaping. Overcoming any **obstacle** in your path. Never stopping. Always moving.

Parkour is an art of movement. It explores the incredible **potential** of your body and your mind.

HISTORY OF PARKOUR

Parkour was created by a group of young men in France in the 1980s and 1990s.

Parkour's first name was "Art du Deplacement". In English, this means the "Art of Displacement".

Displacement means getting from one place to another using only your own body.

The name later changed to parkour.
In the UK, it is also called freerunning.

The **founders** of parkour called their group "Yamakasi".

THREE OF THE YAMAKASI FOUNDERS:

Yann Hnautra

Laurent Piemontesi

Chau Belle-Dinh

Yamakasi is a word from the Lingala language in Africa. It means "strong body, strong spirit".

The group's goal was to become incredibly fit, strong and fast.

They wanted to become people who could meet any challenge.

TRAINING

Parkour is a very difficult activity. It requires lots of training to be able to do it safely and correctly.

The best way to learn is to be taught by experienced instructors.

A parkour instructor teaches a group some basic vaults

Parkour is NOT about **adrenaline** rushes and taking risks. It's quite the opposite!

Parkour is a way of mastering your own movement. It's a way of training your body to achieve its full potential.

You can do much more than you think. Your body and mind can do amazing things when properly trained.

Training is hard, but it's always good fun!

STRENGTH TRAINING

Parkour is about physical fitness and functional strength.

Functional strength means being able to move your body wherever you want to go. This includes being able to climb, run, jump, drop and twist.

You need to prepare your muscles and bones for these movements. This is known as **conditioning**.

The best way to condition your body is to repeat natural, functional movements in the places you are going to be doing parkour.

Parkour also requires regular physical training, such as bodyweight drills.

A bodyweight drill is an exercise that develops your muscles. The exercise uses only the weight of your body, not solid weights.

You must improve your jump strength.

You must also improve your ability to absorb **impact** when you land.

Regular training and building good **technique** should decrease the likelihood of injuring yourself.

JUMPS

There are as many different ways to move in parkour as there are people who train in it!

Parkour has many different types of jumps to learn. These include running jumps, standing jumps, drops and **precision** jumps.

Practitioners of parkour spend long hours practicing how to take off and land well.

They train their legs to absorb the impact of the jump safely and in a controlled way.

Experienced practitioners can make very precise jumps of up to 19.5 feet (almost 6m) in length.

Practicing precision jumping is very important for parkour. You must be able to land in perfect balance on thin or small objects, such as railings or walls.

VAULTS

A vault is a movement that allows you to move over an obstacle and keep going.

A vault is normally used for obstacles that are at chest height.

Most vaults involve jumping over an obstacle while placing your hands on it for control and direction.

The "Saut de Chat" is one type of vault. It means the "jump of the cat". It's a good way to move over low obstacles quickly.

A man doing the Saut de Chat vault

Practitioners dive headfirst over an obstacle.

They place both hands on the obstacle. Then, they bring their knees through their arms.

WALL-RUNNING

A wall-run is a way to get over a very high obstacle or wall.

Practitioners run at a wall.

They place a foot on the wall at about waist height.

Then, they push up while reaching with their arms.

A good wall-run can help practitioners reach the top of a wall that is up to 13 feet (4m) high.

WALL-RUNS ARE VERY EXPLOSIVE MOVEMENTS!

ARM JUMPS

Jumping and grabbing onto an edge, such as the top of a wall, is known as a "Saut de Bras" in French. It means "arm jump" in English.

This move is also known as a "cat leap".

An arm jump is used when a wall or obstacle is too high to jump onto directly.

You must grab the top of the wall with your arms and then pull yourself up.

Arm jumps require a lot of upper body strength.

You can cover huge distances between obstacles using an arm jump.

Training for parkour takes time, so please don't rush!

There are no shortcuts and no secrets – just **discipline**.

MENTAL CHALLENGE

Parkour is far more than just a physical discipline. Parkour challenges the mind in many ways.

You must learn to overcome your fears and inhibitions about movement.

An inhibition is a feeling that stops you from doing something.

You must master your thoughts and learn to focus your attention.

Parkour builds confidence and inner control. It helps you to master yourself.

IN THE PUBLIC EYE

In 2001, there was a movie made called *Yamakasi*. It starred the French founders of parkour.

In the movie, the Yamakasi use their amazing skills to raise money for a young boy who needs an operation.

The movie was filmed in Paris. It showed how parkour can be used to get around a city very fast.

Then, in 2003, a UK **documentary** was released called *Jump London*.

The documentary was filmed all over London. It showed some of London's most impressive buildings and famous places.

Practicing parkour in London

After *Jump London* was released, parkour became huge around the world.

Now, parkour appears in major Hollywood movies.

Parkour was used in the opening scene of the James Bond movie *Casino Royale*.

James Bond chases a villain through a city, and across rooftops and cranes. It was an explosive opening to the movie!

REMEMBER!

The incredible moves you see in movies, magazines and books are performed by trained professionals.

PARKOUR COMPETITIONS

Competitions take place all over the world where freerunners can show off their amazing parkour skills.

In 2018, parkour got its very own World Championships. This is the most exciting parkour competition of all!

The World Championships are held over three days. Freerunners compete against each other on unique and amazing circuits made by world-leading athletes.

In these championships, freerunners showcase their talents in two categories: speed and freestyle. Everyone wants to be crowned the winner!

The World Parkour Championships are set up by the International Parkour Federation (IPF) and the World Freerunning Parkour Federation (WFPF).

There are also other competitions held all over the world.

Parkour competition held in Tel-Aviv, Israel, in 2016

PARKOUR VISION

Learning parkour will completely change your way of seeing the world!

People who train in parkour start to see the world around them differently. They start to think creatively about how they can move from one place to another. They see new ways to use buildings and objects for cool and exciting movements.

They could be moving through a city or a park - every different location is full of possibilities and can inspire new ideas. It makes the world a very exciting place!

With parkour, your **vision** changes completely!

A WAY OF LIFE

For those who train in parkour, it becomes more than just a sport or hobby.

Parkour helps you to improve physically and mentally every day.

Parkour becomes a way of life for its practitioners. They learn that they can overcome problems in their life - not only in training.

LEARNING PARKOUR

If you want to learn parkour, it's best to learn from a qualified teacher or an experienced practitioner.

- All you need to take part are running shoes and simple training clothes, such as sportswear – nothing else!
- Classes always involve tough physical training and lots of repetition of the movements of parkour. It can be hard work!
- You can find information on groups and classes in your community online.

GLOSSARY

adrenaline - a substance produced in the body in response to excitement. It makes your heart beat faster.

conditioning - the process of training your body to improve its strength, movement and muscle control.

discipline - the ability to commit to practicing and training regularly, and with focus.

documentary - a factual TV show or movie.

founder - a person who starts something, such as an organization or a sport.

impact - the force that goes through your body when you land from a jump.

obstacle - a wall, park bench, set of steps – any object you can move over when practicing parkour.

potential - what your mind and body are capable of if you train hard.

practitioner - a person who practices (takes part in) an activity.

precision - being very accurate with your movements and landings from jumps.

technique - a way of doing something.

vault - a movement that allows you to move over an obstacle and keep going.

vision - the ability to see new possibilities for movement in your surroundings.

INDEX

Picture credits:
(t=top; b=bottom; c=center; l=left; r=right):
Shutterstock: Anna Kornak 30; Areporter 20-21, 31b; Gulsrud Visuals 5; Hedry Handoko 26-27; Jacob Lund 20; Krasobski Dmitri 6, 16-17; ReneGamper 18; Rommel Canlas 14, 19, 29br; Standret 1, 13; Urbanscape 2-3; Vagengeium 12b; Wavebreakmedia 10, 29t. Big Pictures: 23c. Parkour Generations: 7l, 7c. Andy Day: 4, 7r, 8, 9, 11t, 11b, 15, 22, 24, 25, 28.